LIVING THE ZEN LIFE

LIVING THE ZEN LIFE

Practicing Conscious, Compassionate Awareness

VOLUME THREE

BY ALEX MILL

Zen Life Books

Zen Life Books
Louisville, CO 80027
www.zenlifebooks.com

Cover photograph: Will van Wingerden

ISBN-13: 978-1-7342391-5-7
ISBN-10: 1-7342391-5-8

CONTENTS

INTRODUCTION

There are hundreds of books about Zen Buddhism, enlightenment, scriptures, religious ceremonies, and esoteric Zen philosophy.

This book isn't one of them.

During my 14 years of training in a Zen monastery, I didn't read books. In fact, when I arrived at the monastery, all of my books, journals, and belongings were confiscated. No reading of any kind was permitted of the monks unless it was a public note posted on the message board or material specifically given to us as part of a workshop. Our bi-weekly group discussions did not focus on gaining more knowledge and we never spoke about our practice objectively. There were no "Dharma talks," so to speak.

So what did I learn about and what on earth did I do while I was there?

I *lived* Zen. Daily. 24/7.

I learned about myself. I was the context, the object, *and* the subject.

Through meditation, service, and the awareness practices offered at the Zen monastery, I discovered my own inner landscape and how to navigate through it. I saw the habitual patterns I repeated, the identities I clung to, the beliefs I cherished, the projections I believed, and the stories I indulged. I observed how I caused myself to suffer so I could see through that suffering and end it. I was in the trenches with myself going through what I now refer to as "Spiritual Bootcamp." It was the most profound experience of my life and one that now inspires me to give back what I have been so generously given.

The stories, lessons, principles, and vignettes in this book are all from my experiences of Zen training. Each chapter begins with an opening quote as an anchor for the subject matter. Periodically, I include cartoons I drew at the monastery to help illustrate concepts. There is no particular organization to the themes, no rhyme or reason, but all do have an underlying premise:

You're either present or not present. Here or not here. Free or suffering.

The voices in our heads talk to us and describe our world to us. They also coerce us into doing what is harmful and discourage us from doing what would be helpful. They see, speak, and act through us in our unconsciousness—if we allow them to.

The ultimate goal in practice, as I learned it, is to awaken beyond these voices and practice staying in conscious, compassionate awareness full time—to self-mentor ourselves to do what serves us, others, and Life the best.

It's what I refer to as *Living the Zen Life*.

It's an ongoing practice with no finish line. A practice for practice's sake. Filled with falling down and getting up. Again and again and again.

Done for the joy of practicing itself.
May you find this joy yourself!

In lovingkindness,

Alex

Dedicated to all my students and clients.
Thank you for making this work possible.

SPENDING ATTENTION

"Thoughts are mental energy; they're the currency that you have to attract what you desire. Learn to stop spending that currency on thoughts you don't want."
—Wayne Dyer

One of the things I embraced while I was training at the Zen monastery was the spirit of conscious, compassionate inquiry. I spent every moment evaluating if what I did supported my practice or if it did not. This inquiry helped most areas of my life, but it was especially valuable to me when it came to money.

As the cook, it helped me determine where our donated funds would go at the grocery store. It helped me see which ingredients were going to be the most in line with our principles. We didn't indulge in processed foods that were expensive, but rather nutritious foods that were cost effective. We chose organic when we knew the conventional options were the most heavily contaminated. We spent our money at the mom-and-pop shops for the bulk of our groceries because supporting our local small businesses was in line with our values.

This attitude of mind carried over to all the other positions I held during my stay at the monastery. When I was the gardener, it helped me determine which produce to grow: What did we eat the most? Where did most of our money go at the store and how could we save it? When I was operating the small business, it helped me determine the type of packaging we used for shipping: Was it made from recycled materials? Could it be entirely recycled on the other end once it was shipped?

You see, conscious, compassionate awareness understands that all of my decisions have consequences. Every good and every bad ripples and perpetuates. *Oneness* doesn't want to harm. It strives for sustainable benefit.

Even today, outside the monastery, I look around me and see what I surround my life with. What do I spend my money on? Where do I invest my attention? When I look around me, I will immediately see what I value. Without judgment, I can start to use what I see as guidance to inform what I want to shift. Is there too much processed food in my diet? Not enough exercise? Not enough fresh air? Did I help someone today? How am I spending my money?

Writing my last book was a huge investment of time, energy, attention, and money. When I left the Zen monastery, I made a vow that I was going to share what made the biggest impact on my life with the world. So this book was going to be my most helpful one yet, filled with some of the most powerful stories and lessons I could remember. I hired and paid an excellent editor thousands of dollars to ensure that *A Shift to Love* was going to be perfect.

In the back of my mind, I had voices yelling at me telling me that all that money was going to go to waste. It would never make back what went into it. But I didn't care. I knew that the reason I was writing that book was to fulfill my mission, and my values were more important to me than anything else.

Again, I look to see if my money is going to what's harmful or to what's helpful.

In this way, my relationship with money mirrors spiritual practice perfectly. In meditation, I am investing all of my attention, energy, and effort into what leads to freedom, while withdrawing my attention, energy, and effort from what causes suffering.

May my spent money serve the same purpose as my spent attention, energy, and effort.

May I continue to make good investments and significant withdrawals.

FOR THE LOVE OF THE UNIVERSE

"To describe myself in a scientific way, I must also describe my surroundings, which is a clumsy way of getting around to the realization that you are the entire universe."
—*Alan Watts*

When I was a kid, I was a bit astonished by the realization that to make something "clean," something else had to get "dirty." For example, my dusting rag was soiled by the dirt I was wiping up, and the water was soiled by the dirt when I washed it. I could follow this progression through any example I found. What was "good" for one was "bad" for the other. Cause really did have an effect. (I was a bit of a young philosopher!)

It was my first memory of considering that all my thoughts, words, and deeds had consequences—something I learned while I was training at the Zen monastery.

The gravity of this concept didn't weigh me down, however, but rather it gave me pause to consider what I was doing before taking action. It encouraged me to practice being as present as I could be all the time. Because if I lapsed and allowed the voices in my head to speak or act through me, it could get quite ugly.

But I didn't want to pause too long to allow those same voices to stop me from doing anything. Waiting too long and going up into my head to consider, "Is this good or bad...?"

could get me into as much trouble as acting without conscious-ness. Soyen Shaku, the first Zen teacher to come to America, described the process in his personal rules for living this way, *"When an opportunity comes do not let it pass by, yet always think twice before acting."*

In this way, I was striving to determine if what was arising in me was insight or ego. A very delicate balance and a razor's edge. I practiced in this way for the love of the universe because what affected me, affected others, and rippled out to all. It wasn't something I wanted to take lightly, but I did want to do it light-heartedly.

PREPARING FOR DEATH

"While I thought that I was learning how to live, I have been learning how to die."
—*Leonardo da Vinci*

One of the most honest responses I've ever heard to the question, "What do you believe happens after death?" came from a spiritual teacher who simply replied, "I don't know. I have not died. I have no experience of death so how could I explain to you what happens after death?"

The truth in that answer struck me. Consider: Who is going to supply you with the information you're looking for? Who is going to know the answers for certain? Who had the experience and (pun intended) "lived to tell about it?"

I'm convinced that every belief we have created around death is to help us feel better about the mystery of it—a mystery that can either leave us with angst or terrify us. So we sock something away into our minds to make sense of our own existence as a way to console us. But a story is still a story.

So how do we practice with death then? A loved one passes away, a pet we care about dies, and we're all going to die too. What can we do about all the thoughts, memories, and feelings we have around this?

Before we tackle "what should you do?" please keep in mind that we typically jump into how to practice with life challenges when something big and difficult comes along—when we're faced with a life challenge. We're diagnosed with a terminal illness, someone we love dies, or we've hit rock bottom and all of a sudden, we need to figure out how to cope. As difficult as this may sound, beginning to practice during these times is the worst time to do it. Why? Because if you haven't been practicing all along, how do you expect to have the foundation you need to deal with this challenge? Picture it: You're out at sea, you've capsized, and you're going under—so *now* you'd like to learn how to swim? My best encouragement to you in this situation is to survive! Just make it through the best you can. Yes, it will be messy, yes it will be tough, yes it will be rugged—but do the best you can.

Zen has been called a practice to prepare us for death. We're cleaning up behind ourselves, and we're creating a situation in which we're not clinging to or pushing anything away. So we can release fully, and we can also be fully present with the process.

My recommendation as you practice is to release all "shoulds" you've been given about how it ought to be. Everything will arise, and your job is simply to observe it all. We've inherited a cultural narrative about what death means, how we should feel about it, and how we should process it. It's not kind or helpful to ourselves to be held to new standards just because we heard there's another way to be with it. That's just turning practice over to the voices to beat us up for how we're doing, which is not the practice.

As with any situation in life, death or otherwise, I would ask you to consider this question, "Are the choices you're making right now leading you toward or away from suffering?" If you can honestly see how you're choosing suffering or freedom in any given moment, it will help you compassionately self-mentor yourself with the love and assistance you need. And that's a powerful tool to have in any situation.

PROBLEMS AND CLUES

"Where there is ruin, there is hope for a treasure."
—Rumi

A problem is simply a clue. It's a clue that more attention is needed, not less.

It's a clue demanding more creativity or conscious, compassionate communication. Like sitting down with the *real* person you're struggling with and doing your best to express your points of view (instead of expressing them with an imaginary person in your head).

Self-hate is a clue that more self-compassion is needed.

Anger is a clue that maybe there was a breach of integrity somewhere (like he said he was going to do something but didn't).

Suffering over feeling alone is a clue that perhaps inviting others may shift the energy.

While feeling helpless is a clue that a proactive, empowered approach may be required.

What if feeling small is a clue that guides you to evoke the part of you who is *big*?

You see, most of the new age approaches to problem-solving I hear these days are the equivalent of whisking them away under the carpet.

"Oh, my partner is so mean to me. That means I should be at peace with it and learn to deal. I need to breathe when I feel the impulse to riot. I have cravings and I know they're the ego, so I need to stop it."

Well, those "solutions" are what happen when the voices get ahold of the teachings, pervert them, and use them to disempower you.

Cravings could be the ego—or they could be clues to crave something beneficial. Put that craving to work! Instead of putting it toward what causes you to suffer, put it toward what creates freedom and good.

Remember, problems are clues to go deeper. They're an opportunity to get super curious. Problems should set your spirit on fire with enthusiasm and wild creativity.

If there isn't any, put your attention there. And search for more clues!

SEEKING GUIDANCE

"Only one person in a million becomes enlightened without a teacher's help."
—*Bodhidharma*

Every so often, I'll run into someone who will disagree with my point that a teacher or a master is essential to proper training. This person will typically argue by saying, "I'm my own guru. I follow my inner wisdom." What I can know is that this is a potentially dangerous person—especially if this person is a teacher.

Blind spots are blind spots precisely because we cannot see them. Most people aren't present enough to catch the majority of them. Stack on top of that the elusive nature of the voices. These voices in our heads think, speak, and act through us without us seeing that they're voices. They just sound like us thinking.

Facilitating monks at the Zen monastery who were leading away workshops would always travel in pairs. At least pairs. The reason for this was because the ego is sneaky and can undermine what happens in the facilitation. Or it can even influence how a monk behaves outside of the workshop. When another set of eyes was present, however, it provided the opportunity for guidance. The hope was that at least one of the monks was awake enough to see the situation from a disidentified point of view. Because all it took was one "better idea" to sabotage the trip: A change in how an exercise was done or some random action that was not part of the plans. There was always a huge risk that the Dharma would be damaged. Guidance was set up to prevent that.

Until we are trained to see, understand, know, and experience all the nuances of how the voices of egocentricity work, it's always best to seek guidance. And even you're trained—seek guidance.

What's the harm? Only the ego would avoid asking for the gift of guidance. Why? Because then it's plans can be thwarted. It might not get the answer it wants. It might not get its way.

A great example of this is "just doing something without asking." You know those situations. We've all been there and done that. You'll be presented with a situation in which it's unclear if it's permissible to do something. The still small voice will suggest that you ask to find out. The voices will quickly interject and say, "Nah, it's probably okay. Don't bug people..." You act on that bad advice. And then what happens? A massive breakdown! You end up bugging people in a very big way by acting without asking. The final result: You get a royal beating in your head from the voices. Or they redirect that beating at others in the form of anger. "Stupid people with their stupid rules..."

How can the concept of guidance be useful to you out in the world? A great place to start is by consciously and compassionately communicating. If you don't know, ask. If you notice you're debating with an imaginary person in your head, talk to the real one. If you think you already know, check in with someone more experienced.

Not always for the answers necessarily, but for the opportunity to bounce around feedback. To shine a light on the voices and give you a chance to take your best step forward.

THE FIRST STEP

"The journey of a thousand miles begins with one step."
—*Lao Tzu*

e don't take ourselves seriously enough where it matters, and we take ourselves waaaaaay too seriously where it doesn't matter.

We're cautiously pushing away what could help us and carelessly accepting what could harm us.

We waste our time with the trivial and blow off the essential.

But this isn't some fatal, terminal, permanent condition. It's just something we've practiced for so long that it has become second nature.

You see, it's easier to blow off everything that would involve us and ask everything from us than to say "Yes" and face down the unknown. That's why they call it Pandora's Box! All hell breaks loose when you take the first step.

But does it really?

In my experience, what actually happens is we get accustomed to taking *the next* step. All of a sudden, the weight from the first one is lifted, and my stepping becomes a skipping. And then a skipping to a dancing! Suddenly, I'm whirling about ecstatically with joy. I'm left wondering what all that silly resistance was about in the first place.

And here's what I've discovered: The degree of resistance I'm experiencing is the degree of freedom and aliveness that's waiting for me on the other side of resistance. Almost always.

But this is hard to see and easy to forget. The insight resets to dread, and we're staring up the wall of fire again.

That's why our wishy-washy lives are in desperate need of a personal trainer, a guide, a coach, a mentor—someone to create non-negotiable agreements with to keep us on track. Someone to help us through to the other side of resistance and beyond. Because it can be a tricky minefield to maneuver through.

We can forget who we authentically are and believe the tape loop of self-hate instead.

I play the role of a guide in people's lives, and I teach people how to play that role in their own lives.

It's a skill most of us have never been taught, and, ironically enough, we've been taught the opposite. We have been conditioned to believe that what we need comes from the outside. Satisfaction, love, acceptance, answers, fulfillment are all *out there*. Out of reach and never quite right or enough.

But just because that's how we see the world now, doesn't mean we can't shift the momentum in the opposite direction.

It takes a step—the tiniest step to set it going. Do it enough, and you'll never want to stop.

Why would you?

LOOKING FOR LOVE

"...And you came knockin' on my heart's door You're everything I've been lookin' for..."
—*Johnny Lee*

Attention and approval are what people crave the most. Consider for a moment everything you do in your day-to-day life. Why are you doing any of it? If you say your priority is getting certain things like more money, go a little deeper. Ask yourself, "What will I have when I get that?"

Pay attention to how children are socialized. Why do they end up doing what they do? What possible motives could they have for their actions?

Some children do everything they can to please and impress others for approval: They'll get good grades in school, become the best on the sports field, or garner popularity with their peers. Others who know that the "being good" role has already been taken, may choose an opposite tactic. They'll decide to get attention by displeasing others: They'll do drugs, get lousy grades, attract the wrong crowd, or smash up cars.

I coached a mother whose son had turned to using and making drugs. He continued to do this because a group of his friends appreciated his creativity and valued what he did. He got the attention and the approval he sought from them instead of his family.

The sad part is most of us are still in this child-like relationship with others. We're all seeking and demanding approval from outside of us and believing in its lack. This relationship is extremely conditional, not particularly helpful, and gets us into all sorts of trouble.

"Looking for love in all the wrong places." Isn't that how the song goes? Maybe it's out there in that person, or in that job, or in that experience.

The myth is—happiness, love, attention, and approval are all out there somewhere. We just need to find them.

It took me some sitting with myself in meditation and a practice I learned at the Zen monastery to discover that my Hero's Journey was in search of what was already inside of me, under my nose. I found that I already was everything I'd been looking for, the attention and the approval I sought was my own, and only I knew how to walk through my heart's door.

YOGA AT 6 A.M.?

"I've been knocked down a lot of times."
—*James Brown*

So here's the scenario...

The night before, I get super-jazzed about doing yoga at 6:00 a.m. (anyone else out there who gets super-jazzed about exercising early in the morning the night before?). I go to bed and set the alarm so I can be sure I don't sleep through my commitment. I pull the covers over me in my warm flannel sheets and snuggle into my pillow with a smile on my face. The star-studded movie of Mighty Me doing rock-solid power yoga in the morning while the sun is on its way up flickers on the screen of my imagination.

It's gonna be good.

Fast forward to 6:00 a.m....with that alarm making a ruckus.

"That %#!!* alarm!!!"

My eyes roll in their sockets, and I curse the fool who thought that getting up out of bed at 6:00 a.m. was going to be a good idea. Oh, and on top of that, I'm supposed to do something as *ridiculous as yoga*!

I sigh and grumble.

After shutting the alarm off, I habitually roll over onto one side and dimly stare into space through crumbly peepers.

And then it happens. The Great Debate and The Bargaining For My Immortal Soul begins:

- You don't really feel like getting up.
- You could do yoga later in the afternoon or tonight.
- Or even tomorrow...
- You just did yoga the other day.
- What are you trying to prove anyway?
- How about yoga every *other* day?
- What difference does it make if you do yoga now or later?
- It's too cold and dark to do yoga. Better to wait until it's warmer and brighter.
- Tomorrow. There's always tomorrow. That's why God created tomorrow.
- Maybe just a few more minutes in this warm, cozy, *comfy* bed and then see how you feel...

Eventually, one of these hook-line-and-sinkers nabs me and lulls me toward the desired outcome—not doing yoga (and, ultimately, feeling bad). Here's how the process goes:

1. The Set-Up
2. The Follow Through
3. The Beating

The "Set-Up" happened the day before with a fantasy of how yoga was going to be. It's the expectation and the promise of perfection.

The "Follow Through" was the resistance that met the commitment. Now notice how there's only resistance to doing something beneficial. If I had committed to eating a box of donuts, drinking a gallon of coffee, or even playing video games first thing in the morning—I would have gotten nothing but "Hey, great idea! Party time!"

But no.

I decided to do something that would take care of me, make me feel good, energize me for the entire day, and probably set a good tone for everything to follow. This sabotage is the reason I call it self-hate. 'Cause the insidiousness of the whole process is that it leads to "The Beating."

Let me rustle up the voices again for you. Here's what "The Beating" has to say:

- Geez, you didn't do yoga again!
- You can't do anything you've committed to!
- And you wonder why your life is crapola?
- You have no discipline!
- What a loser!
- Pathetic!
- When will you *ever* get it right?
- There's no hope for you.
- Why bother?

After spending a sufficient amount time being pounded into the earth—having traded the possibility of doing yoga and feeling good for a morning dose of "Feel Like Dog Doo-Doo'— the following may start to creep in around mid-day:

- You know, you can always do yoga tomorrow...
- That's' right! All is not lost!
- This could be a good time to create that schedule you've always wanted to follow.
- Remember when you made that schedule and you followed it for half-a-day?
- Boy! That was a smokin' half-day!
- Let's do *that* again!
- And put yoga on at 6:00 a.m.!
- Heck, why not 5:00 a.m.? You want to see the sunrise, don't you?

- Heck *yeah!!!*

I hope you can see the cycle back to The "Set-Up."

I'm being set up.

Again!

More expectations, more opportunities for failure, and more feeling bad.

This process always amazes me. I admire the structure of it. It's like a well-oiled machine — a real guarantee for misery.

Look to see what *your* version of this process is. Do you try to lose weight? Do you try to eat healthier foods? Do you try not to shop so much? Do you try to meditate? Whatever it is, see how this shows up for you.

Write out what the voices say:

THE SET-UP

_____

_____

_____

THE FOLLOW THROUGH

_____

_____

_____

THE BEATING

_____

_____

_____

And pay attention to catch any voice that may try to come in to express an opinion about what you're discovering. The voices would *love* to take your insights and use them against you. Why? Because it just keeps the whole thing moving again.

THE SPIRIT OF GENEROSITY

"Doing good holds the power to transform us on the inside, and then ripple out in ever-expanding circles that positively impact the world at large."
—*Shari Arison*

In my experience, generosity becomes a way of seeing and interacting with the world when the illusion of separation has vanished. As fear drops away, authenticity fills the space and becomes our governing spirit.

No me. No you. Just one.

"Harm" affects everything and ripples just as "benefit" affects everything and ripples.

Children are children. Not my children or your children. Just children.

Everything.

The world becomes quite precious from this perspective.

Even the way we treat an inanimate object like a box or a stamp on a letter becomes a mirror for how we view ourselves and the world.

The Karma bead in my rosary states: "I am born of Karma, I am heir to Karma, I abide in Karma, and I am supported by Karma. Whatever I do creates Karma, and I shall surely experience this Karma. The merit of all good acts I do freely offer to all sentient beings."

What I love about this recitation is that in speaking it out loud I am acknowledging interconnectedness (or better, *oneness*. Interconnected still suggests separation). Everything I think, say, and do is inescapable and, likewise, is forever being created and made anew. Which is why I love the last part of the Karma bead's assertion, "The merit of all good acts I do freely offer to all sentient beings." To me, this means that if I'm going to make my bed and lie in it—I might as well vow to make a darn good bed!

Doing good and living a harmless life seem to make a lot more sense when seen through these lenses.

And we do see this generosity in glimpses out in the world. Generosity is in those touching videos that go viral. You know the ones. They usually have a person or an animal doing something for the sake of another. Our hearts open and we say, "Gosh. I wish there were more of this out in the world. The world would be a much better place if we all acted like this."

We nod and understand. Yet when push comes to shove, it can be so challenging to access this *oneness*. For one thing, since we were children, the illusion of separation has been following us like a shadow that will never leave. We've been trained to experience fear, loss, lack, and deprivation. Without the conditioned tape loop running in our heads to remind us that "the world is the way it is," we'd suddenly see it the way it truly is.

In my experience, the entrance to generosity begins with meditation. A time to see through the delusion that creates the separation. A time to train the attention to come back to *now*. A time to sit in silence and simply *be*.

Meditation opens your life. It's the first crack in the door to let the light in. When the light comes in, it becomes easier to see what's what. And when that happens, you see that it shines on all of us equally. We're all in this together.

YOU EVERYWHERE

"Life is a mirror and will reflect back to the thinker what he thinks into it."
—*Ernest Holmes*

Other people are a golden opportunity to see ourselves more clearly.

Where we all miss, is we play the game of seeing others as different from ourselves and trying to change them. We want them to mirror our best selves, and stop mirroring what we cannot stand or repress about ourselves.

"Mirror" is the keyword. We have a problem with others because the filter in our heads is constantly evaluating them based on our own beliefs and assumptions. What we don't realize is that we're projecting our own voices, standards, meanings, and evaluations onto them.

Here's a little exercise to see how projection works:

Find someone you admire. Now, come up with three adjectives to describe this person.

Next, find someone you dislike. Now, come up with three adjectives to describe that person.

Now look over your adjectives. What did you come up with? Spend some time with them and inquire deeply. If you do, you will learn a great deal about yourself because every one of those adjectives is *you*. If you can see that, the spiritual game now becomes not how others are different from you, but rather how they are exactly like you.

Some people will complain, "But I'm *not* like that. I would never allow myself to be like that." That's a very big clue, right? Somehow you're being held back from being a certain way because the voices would punish you if you ever fell out of character with how you ought to be. The truth is, you sometimes sneak that way of being in permissible situations. Or in ways the voices justify as being okay.

I once coached a woman who worked at a company for many years and was never promoted. She was triggered because another newer employee suddenly asked for a promotion and received it. The adjectives she used to describe the employee were "pushy, arrogant, and domineering." When we explored these, she could see that she would never do what this woman did because of the inner judgment she'd get if she tried. The voices would call her pushy, arrogant, domineering, and worse!

I then asked her if she thought that employee would call herself those adjectives. She smiled. Obviously, she wouldn't. So I asked her if she wouldn't use those adjectives, which ones would she use to describe herself?

So she started to inquire. Instead of "pushy," she saw that this woman was unafraid of asking for what she wanted. So perhaps "assertive." Good! How about arrogant? Again, the word "confident" seemed more accurate. "Domineering?" She laughed and said, "Um…good leader." More laughter.

Enlightenment!

Then, we did the only thing worthwhile at this point. We committed to work on helping her become assertive, confident, and a good leader.

In a magic shift, her projections became the vehicle for shaping the coaching work we would do together. We helped her build her skills so she could get more of what she wanted and end the pattern of being held back. She saw how the voices put a negative spin of being powerful, and this would just not do if she were going to become successful.

There's a lot of talk about how you should use "negative" things that happen to you as opportunities for growth, but there's not much mention about *how* to do that. Projection is a wonderful tool to keep in your back pocket as a way to learn more about yourself. When you use it in a non-judgmental way, it can facilitate real change for you from the inside-out.

"It is not the man who has little, but he who desires more, that is poor."
—Seneca

D esire.

Don't confuse *desire* with *have*.

If you have a lot or if you have a little, it doesn't matter. If you are present and experience non-separation, you are rich.

It's those who *desire* more, or less, who experience separation and therefore suffering.

Desire makes you poor because according to the voices in your head, you'll never have enough and circumstances will never be right enough.

So have or have not, it is irrelevant. Be here and be a king.

ACCEPTANCE IS

"The first step toward change is awareness. The second step is acceptance."
—*Nathaniel Branden*

You are not at war with the mind. The mind is not something to be "shut off." The thing that is at war with the mind is your problem. You identify with this illusion because you can. It carries you along for the ride like a hijacked passenger.

You're not learning how the voices in your head work so you can do something about them. You're not fighting to get rid of them. You're not in a battle to convert them into positive ones. You're also not turning away from them and burying your head in the sand.

What you are learning is this: Your relationship with the voices is what keeps them real.

You're not leaving goals, hard work, self-sacrifice, busyness, and hustle in exchange for peace, bliss, ease, relaxation, and fun. Those are two sides of a duality that bind you to the world of the conditional. The voices would love to have you swing back-and-forth from wrong to right and good to bad, so you believe that your well being is dependent on circumstances. As long as you assume one is preferable—you're lost.

So you stay at war. You are fooled by the hard work to change or the passive resignation of quietism. Both miss the mark.

Acceptance is an end to all of that. Acceptance is awareness. It is not analysis. Awareness sits and observes all that arises regardless of what arises. It really doesn't matter what you see. It's that you see.

In seeing, acceptance is. And with acceptance, freedom.

RELATIONSHIPS AND PROJECTION

"It ain't what you don't know that gets you into trouble. It's what you know for sure that just ain't so."
—Mark Twain

One of the most helpful awareness practice tools that can aid us in relationships is projection.

Projection is nothing more complicated than, "what you see is who you are." When you begin to pay close attention and do some deep spiritual work, you'll realize how much of an assumption it is to believe that there's an objective reality "out there" in which something is "true."

Take a room full of people, and you'll see that they all have their own ideas about what "truth" is. This truth ranges from what is good taste, what styles are favorable, what's moral, what's important in life, etc.

You can narrow that down to just two people, and you'll begin to see the same phenomenon. Maybe it's your life partner or a family member. You're not the same, right? It's really quite fascinating (or startling!) to get it that you don't objectively see life.

For the sake of spiritual practice, if you start to look inward, you'll realize that all it takes is *you* to begin the contradictions. One moment you're identified with a happy-go-lucky spirit, and in the next, you're identified with a strict, by-the-books spirit.

You can feel close and connected to people in one moment and want to hit them in a rage in the next. In this way, "what you see is who you are" can help you determine who you're identified with inside of you—which aspect of your personality is up in any given moment.

Complicate all of this further by throwing in some voices that interject opinions, judgments and self-hate into the mix, and you'll see that "you" are in flux as much as (if not more than) life is. Nothing is stapled down or "real," and who you think you are is a complete and utter fiction made up by the narrative that goes on in the background of your consciousness.

In fact, when people get present to how much of an influence the voices have over their lives, they're typically left stunned and speechless. You see, the voices translate the world we experience into the meaning we carry around with us. They are our full-time simultaneous interpreters.

The idea of the voices as simultaneous interpreters became the inspiration for a cartoon I drew while I was at the monastery. This cartoon offers a graphic representation of how life is filtered by our projections, beliefs, assumptions, and voices.

If you've ever been in situations where you've repeatedly drawn the same conclusions that seem real, chances are good you're buying into a story that *The Simultaneous Interpreter* is telling you. This insight is a golden opportunity to take a step back and question the authority in your head. Understand that everything you experience is a *projection* coming from *you* and the only thing you ever get to experience is *yourself*.

41

TEACHING ME TO LOVE

"Love is the answer, and you know that for sure; Love is a flower, you've got to let it grow."
—*John Lennon*

I had a big laundry list of things wrong with me.

This list sparked my obsession with becoming a personal development project. I was going to finally turn myself into the ideal human I knew I could be.

There's a big trend in that right now. Big headlines that read, "become the person you have the potential to be." It's really quite glamorous. Full of productivity and bio hacks, positive mindsets and activities.

After spending my time visioning, I knew exactly what the person I could be looked like. I knew how he would talk, the kinds of things he'd accomplish, the thoughts he'd have in his head, the feelings he'd have in his body, the relationships he'd have in his life, and the way he'd see the world. Oh, and most importantly, how others would see him.

I had a sobering moment looking at who I was, and this sickening dread fell over me. I got angry at the miserable person I really was who was holding me back from becoming perfect. All these flaws. It just seemed insurmountable and unfair.

And then, in a moment of intuitive grace, while I was writing something in my journal and caught my reflection in the mirror, I finally understood what the practice had been teaching me. My eyes opened to the parts of me I despised. I realized that they were despised by the voices of self-hate—and that self-hate was not me. These small, innocent parts of me who have been downtrodden since I was a kid opened my heart to compassion. I saw how they were bullied and on the receiving end of constant abuse—kicked while they were down, made fun of, discouraged, and shamed.

With my heart wide open, I remarked at how these "poor, pathetic souls" were really my saviors. The sinners I was taught to hate were actually saints, and they were teaching me how to love unconditionally.

The irony was, I owed them my life. They were my doorway to saving myself disguised as damnation. From that moment going forward, I knew that my salvation laid in extending compassion to the targets of greed, hate, and delusion. Wherever compassion was missing, it was my job to bring it. Whatever was wrong, was suddenly made right through my own love.

COMPOUNDED THOUGHTS

"I've been putting out the fire with gasoline."
—David Bowie

Imagine you set up an email auto-reply to forward incoming emails to another email address. Then imagine you set that second email address up with an auto-reply forwarding emails back to the first address. What happens? You create an endless loop of emails bouncing back and forth to each other.

That's what's going on inside the mind when it's lost in discursive thought.

Judgment arises. Then judgment arises to judge the judgment. Then feeling bad arises for the judgment of the judgment.

Every thought compounds the previous one needlessly with no benefit whatsoever.

"You weren't paying attention. That's why this happened."

"Not paying attention is bad."

"You should pay attention more."

"What's wrong with you for not paying attention?"

Smack!...

Right into a pole. You were listening to the voices banter on about not paying attention when you should have been

..paying attention.

A PRINCIPLE FOR CLARITY

"Begin challenging your assumptions. Your assumptions are the windows on the world. Scrub them off every once in awhile or the light won't come in."
—*Alan Alda*

You can find wisdom in anything; because when something is said out of context, you can make a case for it being true. But context is everything. Without having all the information, you can't make a centered decision.

My teacher used to express her frustration with the monks when one of us would show up to her for guidance. We'd ask her how to proceed on a particular issue and leave out some important detail. The monk would explain everything, she'd make a decision, and then the monk would say, "Oops. So sorry. No, I'm sorry...that would not be a good course of action because I forgot to tell you about this detail..." With any luck, that would solve it. But I've overheard several conversations in which the poor monk continued to say "Oops!" only to have my teacher grit her teeth and wonder if the whole story would ever get out.

I can see the same phenomenon occur on the other end—with the monks. Guidance would get pulled out of context and suddenly we would start saying, "But the guidance I received was to always use two pans in the oven." Now the monks have inadvertently created a rule out of a contextual incident that may or may not apply to the current situation. And we'd continue to use it.

It could be months down the line when my teacher shows up in the kitchen and asks me, the Cook, "Why on earth are you using two pans in the oven?" I'd shrug my shoulders and explain to her that the guidance I received was that this is how we're doing it from now on. By the look on her face, I could tell that this was the wrong answer (and another out-of-context guidance decision made into rule that leads to breakdowns).

Assumption, lack of clarity, and failure to understand the context is what creates sabotage in communication. Oftentimes, a simple understanding of the principle behind the guidance could fix everything. For example: Two pans in the oven when you're attempting to achieve x. Now, with the reason and the underlying principle from which the decision was made, everyone can move forward confidently. We now know how the guidance was arrived at and when it is applicable.

This is the practice and the aim we're striving for. It's what happens when we speak from Center and understand that context is important as we avoid assumptions, which then lead to breakdowns.

Conscious, compassionate, communication makes for clarity. A wonderful principle to practice.

A TIME AND A PLACE

"Good things come to those who wait."
—*Violet Fane*

"Carpe Diem! (Seize the day!)"
—*Horace*

So what's it going to be?

Now or never? Or lifetimes? Will you practice like your hair's on fire? Or will you be casual about it?

One of my favorite mentors, Steve Chandler, used a perfect distinction to teach the coaches in his school. He said, "I can be serious in my profession, but I don't have to take myself seriously."

In this simple statement, he made it obvious that seriousness has a time and a place. In one instance, being serious is necessary to produce success and, in the other, detrimental to it.

The same is true with spiritual practice. I take my practice extremely seriously. Staying conscious is a non-negotiable way of being and living life. It's not something stapled to my to-do list. I am not practicing for the sake of attaining results. In fact, seeking an enlightened ego keeps me blind to the simple task of being present.

Ironically, the moment I'm a somebody is the moment I'm lost.

So our focus in practice? Be going as fast as you can when end up falling on your face!

WHAT DOESN'T WORK

"Jealousy works the opposite way you want it to."
—Lululemon

In the world of conditioned mind, up is down and black is white. What the voices in our heads talk us into doing is typically counter to what would be in our best interest. That's why learning to discern the voices from the "still small voice" of intuition is so important.

This understanding also applies in circumstances outside of ourselves—in relationship with others.

I was once coaching a client who relayed the following story. She told me about her husband and how he had become completely withdrawn and uninterested in her. After a series of questions, what surfaced was she had resorted to confrontation to get the love she wanted from him. This included accusing, nagging, blaming, shaming, and even threatening him. In the coaching, I gently revealed why this approach would never help her get the love she was looking for from him. I drew out my "cat analogy" to illustrate this point.

I asked her to imagine a cat hiding under a chair. "Now," I said to her, "imagine that you're yelling at the cat. You're hoping that this will encourage it to come out from under the chair and cuddle with you. All your anger isn't working so you get louder. Now the cat is even more resistant to coming out.

So you throw something at the chair. Bam! Sure the cat may come out now, but it will not be in a cuddling mood!"

She laughed and understood: Nobody warms up to a crazy person. In fact, this tactic provokes from him more of the same behavior that originally upset her. Her husband became more withdrawn and less interested in being with her the more she fought. To help her stay conscious to this process, she eventually called it "porcupining." She added "not to porcupine her husband" to her agenda, because really, who wants to cuddle with a porcupine? She got it.

So what to do instead? In my experience, cats (and partners) enjoy a loving, welcoming, hospitable, and cuddle-able environment. If you create this space, they'll suddenly feel safe. Because there's nothing more inviting than someone at ease with themselves and not desperately trying to get something from you. It's when you practice love, generosity, kindness, self-fulfillment, confidence, and completeness that others become attracted to you. They crawl out from under their chair and curl up into your lap.

Now there's no guarantee that this approach will produce the results you're looking for. Those are merely by-products of how you are being.

Often, clients will discover that not needing love to come from the outside will become fulfillment enough. They'll focus instead on their projects, goals, and dreams. They'll focus on their friends, children, and communities. It's too distracting to bother dragging someone else along for the ride. And do you know what? At that point, it really doesn't matter. Their partners will either join in with their energy because that's where the party is happening or they'll find their own way. Either is fine.

THE FACE OF FREEDOM

"If you know the enemy and know yourself, you need not fear the result of a hundred battles. If you know yourself but not the enemy, for every victory gained you will also suffer a defeat. If you know neither the enemy nor yourself, you will succumb in every battle."
—Sun Tzu

Understanding when you're identified with the illusion is the first step to popping out of it. Often times, it's the entire journey to freedom itself.

I'll never forget the story about the cook at the Zen monastery (before I became the cook) who said, outloud, in the kitchen, "I'm identified." Being identified, at my monastery where I trained, was code for "stuck in suffering." It means I'm frustrated, angry, upset, fighting something, believing something, or caught up in feeling bad. It's the "trapped as the actor in the play" position in which you don't realize you're the actor in the play. You just believe you're truly the person and what's happening to you is real. When the cook announced that she was stuck, it not only extricated her from suffering but it reinforced her chances of doing it again. Now she could see when the illusion was attempting to keep her in the story and that she could disidentify from it at will. This skill is what we're practicing to master: Closing the gap between suffering and freedom by training our our attention to stay where we want it.

The good news is your desire to be free belongs to the face of freedom staring back at you across the abyss. The moment you see through the illusion is the moment you become that which you are looking for. Where you are going suddenly becomes where you are. Presence meets itself as it cuts through the fog of delusion and dissipates it to the winds. Suddenly, in a great knowing, you are once again home with nowhere left to go, or do, or be.

Awakening is a recognition. You are recognizing authenticity and it becomes a reunion with what is already inside of you. When you are caught up in a challenging inner story you simply forget. You experience yourself as separate from grace. So you begin to develop a longing for it. You want something that you believe is out there somewhere. But you wouldn't know to go looking for freedom if you weren't already experiencing it from within. That's the irony of spiritual practice. There's nowhere to go, nothing to do, and no one to be.

Practice is about remembering your real face.

THE HUNT

"You wander from room to room Hunting for the diamond necklace That is already around your neck!"
—*Rumi*

Life for most people is like an Easter egg hunt.

We're dropped here on this planet, brainwashed to believe that happiness and fulfillment are somewhere hidden and out of reach somewhere, and then we're left to go figure out how to get it. So we scramble about day-in and day-out looking, trying, and efforting until the day we die. If we get close, or if we get a few items checked off from our list, satisfaction may last a few moments, but then we're off to the next great chase. "What I got was okay, but perhaps there's something better over there!"

Now, this is a very good arrangement for the voices in your head. From their perspective, keeping you distracted and busy with the chase is as good as it gets. The drama keeps you suffering, and your suffering is exactly the kind of energy they enjoy siphoned off. A suffering smoothie for them to slurp after a long, hard day of guiding your attention about. So your life force is sucked away—leaving you drained and the voices well fed. As long as they fool you into playing the game, you're their property.

Then, by some chance, along comes meditation. You've heard it's good for you. People are talking about it and how it works to clear the busy mind. And the people who are practicing it suggest that you sit down. Sit down and remain silent. Look inward. Breathe. Focus all of your attention on the breath.

And then what happens?

Perhaps it's pleasant in the beginning. But eventually the voices freak out. They go to work to sabotage your practice. They jabber on, scream, whisper, discourage, and distract. Maybe they'll even have a hand at causing you to "forget" your practice. You've listened to them and believed them for so long, you listen to their frustration and irritation and assume it is your own. You listen to their excuses and complaints and nod your head in agreement. So you may, or may not, continue to meditate. Perhaps for a bit, and then quit.

Or maybe you play the Easter egg hunt again. Except this time, you play it with "find the right meditation and spiritual practice." You look here, there, and everywhere for the right practice for "you." One that will suit you. The one you like. The one that's least threatening. Scrambling about from retreats to yoga studios to temples to programs...never finding anything quite right. The frantic search for peace continues and the voices are quite happy with this arrangement as well. See them gleefully rubbing their hands? This is how they fold spiritual practice and meditation into the worldly objectives that you must attain and obtain to experience happiness and fulfillment. More conditional happiness. More hunting.

When all that was required was for you to sit down. In silence.

A PEACEFUL MIND

"All experience is preceded by mind,
Led by mind,
Made by mind.
Speak or act with a corrupted mind,
And suffering follows
As the wagon wheel follows the hoof of the ox.
All experience is preceded by mind,
Led by mind,
Made by mind.
Speak or act with a peaceful mind,
And happiness follows
Like a never-departing shadow."
—The Buddha, (from The Dhammapada, translated by Gil Fronsdal)

The world is created through the context of your self-talk. When I say "self-talk," I'm referring to the constant stream of unconscious voices in your head that play on without you. They are assessing, analyzing, deducting, drawing meaning, and evaluating everything. They are the filter through which life passes before it reaches you. They present the world to you in a way that makes your experience of life consistent and intelligible to you, according to the structure you live within.

The nature of this conditioned mind, which was created during childhood to socialize you, is mired in "something wrong/not enough." Why? You were taught to abandon who you authentically were in exchange for what you needed so that you can become fit into society. It left you with the psychological premise, "I am wrong. Something is wrong. I need to change to fit in because what is wrong is somehow my fault." The very nature of being conditioned implies this assumption. Why would you be conditioned if all was okay the way you were? So there's no escape for anyone. It's a tough transition for all children—one that is unconsciously perpetuated through the generations and leaves us a byproduct of this process.

Your experience of the world can be summed up as nothing more than you staring directly at a mirror reflecting the posters, snippets, and fictions of the conditioned wallpaper lining the inside of your head. Yet we all walk around through life as though there is some objective truth to be experienced and a "right" way to proceed based on that truth.

My own insight into conditioned mind occurred while I was sitting in meditation at the Zen monastery one day. Suddenly I heard the thoughts start in about how "everybody at the monastery" hated me. Let's take a step back for a moment. Here I was, minding my own business, counting my breath, sitting facing a blank white wall, and the story of "everybody hates me" passes through as clear as day. Keep in mind, nothing was going on. No one was actively saying anything to me me (it was a silent monastery) and yet somehow the feeling that "everyone (at a compassionate Zen monastery) hated me."

Absurd. Unbelievable. Obviously untrue.

Yet completely real to me.

My realization made it extremely clear to me why this work is so vitally important on many levels. One, people, for the most part, are oblivious to this deep inner way of experiencing the world. We look out at it with our own two eyes and assume what we're seeing is true. Two, I was in a Zen monastery where I was training so that I could have this shift—and it's an extremely challenging perspective to attain. Three, the world is being destroyed by our identification with the illusion of a separate self. This delusion must be addressed and can no longer be ignored. We cannot address the pandemic issues the planet faces while failing to see that the very system that created these issues exists within us. The conditioned monster of our mind is working to stomp its image over all the world. If we don't work from the inside out, nothing we do will sustainably rid ourselves of it.

It takes practice to pull the background of our minds to the foreground and recognize what corrupts and what is peaceful—and to choose the one that brings happiness.

THE ANTI-COACH

"When someone beats a rug, the blows are not against the rug, but against the dust in it."
—Rumi

At the monastery where I trained, we had a saying that went something like this:

"If you had people in your life that treated you as badly as the voice in your head treats you, you would have gotten rid of them a long, long time ago."

Many folks have mentors, coaches, personal trainers, and loved ones who support them. Lord knows we could use one inside our own heads!

We pull through for others—we're even kind and compassionate to complete strangers like the grocery clerk—yet when it comes to ourselves, we're left with this crappy, annoying, fear-driven, constantly dissatisfied, whiny voice that berates and puts us down all day long.

Then, when it gets tired of us, it goes on to others. Have you noticed? It's an equal opportunity abuser!

So remember, if you're feeling bad, chances are good The Anti-Coach has whooshed into your life and left you a little something in your punch bowl. Time to fling it into the fan and take back your life!

HAPPY MEANINGLESSNESS

"Nothing makes any sense. Nothing means anything. You're born, you live, you die. That's it."
—*Rachel Ward*

Meaninglessness from the voices and the Dark Room=Cynicism. "Why bother?" Might as well end it all. Everything is pointless." It represents a passive victim point of view.

Meaninglessness from Center and the Light Room = Possibility. "Oh boy! What can I create?! If nothing means anything, then why not create whatever I want?" Why not enjoy the process? Everything is a game. It represents the enthusiastic and the active, creative point of view.

Everything has at least two sides and two ways to be approached. It's up to us to see them both and choose the one that leads to happy meaninglessness.

THEN IT'S GONE

"...form is emptiness, emptiness is form;
emptiness is not separate from form,
form is not separate from emptiness;
whatever is form is emptiness,
whatever is emptiness is form."
—Excerpted from The Heart Sutra (translated by Red Pine)

Nothing is permanent. If you pause for too long, you'll miss it.

There is no foreground and no background. There is nothing to leave and no destination. Therefore no transition. Nothing superfluous. Nothing insignificant or unworthy of your attention.

The Zen view in architecture is a window placed in a hallway or stairwell in which the glorious spectacle is visible only in passing. You can't stand there and take it in for as long as you'd like. It's in sight and then it's gone.

Like an entire lifetime. There in a moment.

WHAT TO SEE

"The best teachers are those who show you where to look but don't tell you what to see."
—*Alexandra K. Trenfor*

Every year at the monastery, we would offer a Precepts retreat. During that retreat, we would explore Buddhism's ten grave prohibitive precepts. These were tenants The Buddha laid down to help guide people away from suffering. The claim was that if you were engaging in any one of them, there was a good chance you were suffering.

People arrived bright-eyed and confident. Many heard "Not to kill, not to drink, not to steal, not to lie, etc." and would interpret them like many interpret The Holy Bible's Ten Commandments "Thou shalt not..." But we did not make it that easy for retreatants. The precepts are not part of a spiritual checklist. "I didn't kill anyone this year—*check!* I didn't drink alcohol this year—*check!*..." Instead, we invited retreatants to explore, "Not to lead a harmful life nor to encourage others to do so." Hmmm. "What *is* harmful? How do *you* define harmful? How do *you* lead a harmful life? How do *you* encourage others to do so? What would it look like not to lead a harmful life—*for you?*"

We went deep into this exploration. Not for answers. Not for "right" or "wrong." "Good" or "bad." But rather to see what there was to see about how we caused ourselves to suffer so we could drop that and end suffering.

That would certainly be a good start.

THERE IS NO RUSH

"Success is not final, failure is not fatal. It's the courage to continue that counts."
—Winston Churchill

Even The Buddha practiced until the day he died. There is no destination. Success isn't the end. Death may, in fact, be the end. It's what you do between now and then that counts.

My story is not the typical "success story." I wasn't down-and-out, hooked on drugs or alcohol, depressed and miserable. In fact, my story was the exact opposite. I felt like I had everything I should in order to be happy. I had the perfect job, the perfect partner, the perfect home, the perfect life. By all rights, I should have been happy and satisfied. But I wasn't. And that's what drove me to train in a Zen monastery. I needed to figure out how to fill the bottomless hole inside of me that could never be filled.

I didn't always succeed. Being a monk was not easy. I struggled a lot. But I found the courage to continue.

I was coaching a client who admitted that he needed to see things a few times before he understood the process behind how he was struggling. I laughed and told him that I was very thick-headed and it took me seeing the same thing hundreds of times before I learned the process!

So there's no rush.

Having the spirit of inquiry and the joy of learning is so incredibly helpful in life. It's what allows you to see setbacks as springboards to possibilities. Things that aren't going your way are happy-blessed-mistakes. Life happening in its own way is a wondrous mystery and game to be played full out.

For the sheer joy of it!

WHERE'S THE JOY?

"Happiness is not a station to arrive at, but a manner of traveling."
—*Margaret Lee Runbeck*

One of the most astonishing discoveries I made during my Zen training was that I could be crying in sadness and experience happiness at the same time. I could also be yelling with anger and be happy. I could be experiencing any emotion at all with full consciousness instead of getting swept into the habitual drama of it.

A question I learned to ask was, "Where's the joy?" Because life *is* joy. If I wasn't experiencing joy, I was encouraged to go looking for it. To ask myself, "Where's the joy?" and to discover what I was doing instead of residing in joy.

In this way, happiness became a way of living rather than a state to achieve. Instead of hoping it would randomly occur due to circumstances, I became the creator of my own happiness *regardless* of the circumstances.

EVERY MOMENT IS THE GURU

"Life always gives us exactly the teacher we need at every moment. This includes every mosquito, every misfortune, every red light, every traffic jam, every obnoxious supervisor (or employee), every illness, every loss, every moment of joy or depression, every addiction, every piece of garbage, every breath. Every moment is the guru."
—*Charlotte Joko Beck*

I was in a conversation with a client and we were talking about the voices in our heads. I told him the good news and the bad news about the voices. I started with the bad news. I told him that the voices never go away. On the other end of the phone, I could hear him gasp. Then, I told him the good news: The voices are our greatest allies. They motivate us to stay present, awake and alert. Because if we don't stay centered, we get swept under their control and lost in their dramas.

Therefore the object of the game is to learn everything we can about the voices. How they work. What they say. When they arise. How they create resistance. How we get fooled by them. Everything.

Now, this approach is counter to the advice we are given about how to deal with our thoughts. We are told we need to control them. We are told we need to focus on the positive. We are told to quiet our minds. Or we are told that thoughts are just thoughts. We sweep them under the rug, never examine them and avoid them at all costs.

I don't encourage any of that. Why have that kind of relationship with an illusion? If you know that you're dealing with an unhelpful thought, why give it that kind of power over you? Instead, acknowledge it, understand it, and learn about it. This so you can never be fooled by it again. When you're clear about the multifarious ways it causes you to suffer, you can simply stop believing it. That's when you begin using the enemy as your spiritual opportunity for awakening.

In consciousness, the voices are our tools. In unconsciousness, we are tools for the voices.

Every moment is our opportunity to see what we are choosing: Suffering or freedom.

THERE IS NO PATH

"Traveler, there is no path, you make the path as you walk."
—*Antonio Machado*

No one ever knows the answers for you because no one has ever been you before.

This is why after all has been said and after every piece of advice has been given and after every encouragement has been made—*you* must make the path as you walk.

Even if you believe you are following in another's footsteps, look again—there is your own gait, your own dance, your own skip and shuffle. *you* are in all of it.

And if you feel like you've "been there and done that before," look again—you've never been in this moment before because every moment is fresh and brand new. *You* are fresh and brand new.

So with these eyes that are free again, where will you walk?

THE NEXT STATE

"Life is a process of becoming, a combination of states we have to go through. Where people fail is that they wish to elect a state and remain in it. This is a kind of death."
—*Anaïs Nin*

I see this all the time with people assuming life is about getting what they want. "If things aren't going *my* way," people think, "then there must be something wrong."

In my experience, everything that happens is our opportunity to see how to become free. Life is a combination of challenges, possibilities, and insights all designed to open us up.

There is no finish line. There is no "over that." There is no "made it."

There is only this current state of growth in front of us on our way to becoming our next state of growth in front of us.

If we aren't growing, we're dead.

TWO CHILDREN

"Rest and self-care are so important. When you take time to replenish your spirit, it allows you to serve others from the overflow. You cannot serve from an empty vessel."
—*Eleanor Brownn*

So many people believe that sacrificing themselves is what service is all about. Mothers, especially, proclaim that they put themselves last and tend to everyone else's needs first. They work to please others and sometimes never even make it onto the list. I wish they could see the real message they are sending to their children and families: Everyone else matters but me. That's what others are taking away from all your effort. Because children don't learn what you tell them. They learn by watching you. By your example. They're becoming what you're role modeling for them. If you are overworked, uncared for, stressed, resentful, self-sacrificing, fake-happy, miserable, and complaining—that's what you're teaching your children to become. It's what they will do when they become adults with children of their own. Now the question is, "Do you want that?"

Obviously not.

Here's the alternative: Take a step back and acknowledge that you no longer want to take this approach. Working hard, being generous, expressing love, and even being a little cranky are all fine—as long as you practice mindfully, compassionately working with yourself to do this from conscious awareness. Because let's face it, you're going to lose your temper. It's not about being a "perfect parent." (Remember: You're instilling the self-hating demands of perfectionism onto others by indulging it). What you want to model instead is a conscious, flesh-and-blood parent who is working to compassionately self-mentor herself. To remind her that it's okay to lose her cool. To reassure her that you'll be me more considerate of her needs. To reassure her that you'll do whatever it takes to make sure she's taken care of too.

So for every person you care for, remember that you have one extra person with you to include. When you have a child, you actually have two: The child in your arms and the child within you.

No one left out.

ABOUT THE AUTHOR

Alex Mill is a Zen Life Coach. He trained in a Zen monastery for nearly 14 years and now offers his extensive experience to help people transform their lives and businesses from the inside-out through mindfulness, meditation, and compassionate self-mentoring practices.

He is the creator of two life-changing, 30-day online retreats, *Heart-to-Heart: Compassionate Self-Mentoring* and its sequel, *Help Yourself to Change.*

He offers an online version of his Zen meditation workshop entitled, *Taming Your Inner Noise,* where you can learn how to meditate and experience why meditation is so important.

He is the author of four other books on Zen awareness practice: *Practicing Presence, Meditation and Reinventing Yourself, The Zen Life: Spiritual Training for Modern Times,* and *A Shift to Love: Zen Stories and Lessons by Alex Mill.*

If you'd like to learn more about Zen Life Coaching, please go to his website, coaching.zenlife.coach, and send an email requesting more information.

Alex lives in Louisville, Colorado with his partner in compassionate transformation, Karen Davis, and their English Crème Retriever, the aggressive cuddler, Prince Jax, Master of All He Surveys (Jax for short).

You can read more about Alex's books, retreats, workshops and latest offerings at www.zenlife.coach.

Practicing Presence

The Zen Life: Spiritual Training
for Modern Times

Meditation and Reinventing Yourself

A Shift to Love: Zen Stories and
Lessons by Alex Mill

Read the other books from this series...

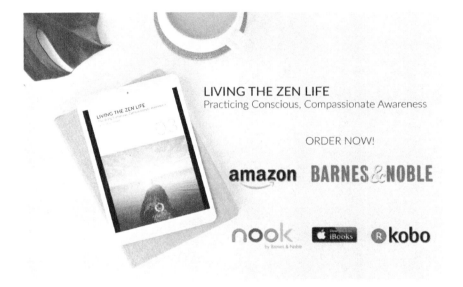

PROGRAMS BY ALEX MILL

- Taming Your Inner Noise: A Zen Meditation Workshop

- Heart-to-Heart: Compassionate Self-Mentoring

- Help Yourself to Change

Get sample chapters from *A Shift to Love...*

SAMPLE.ZENLIFE.COACH

Printed in Great Britain
by Amazon

44154742R00059